A YEAR OF SELF-DISCOVERY

A YEAR OF

Self-Discovery

DAILY PROMPTS TO INSPIRE REFLECTION AND HELP YOU EMBRACE YOUR TRUE SELF

TANYA J. PETERSON, MS, NCC

ROCKRIDGE
PRESS

Series Designer: Alyssa Nassner
Interior and Cover Designer: Lisa Forde
Art Producer: Maya Melenchuk
Editor: Carolyn Abate
Production Editor: Nora Milman
Production Manager: Lanore Coloprisco

Author photo courtesy of Shanna Chess
All illustrations used under license from Shutterstock

Paperback ISBN: 978-1-63807-657-5
eBook ISBN: 978-1-63878-274-2
R0

TO MY YOUNG ADULT "KIDS."
Observing you, I am inspired
to continue to be the best version
of myself. Never stop discovering
and embracing who you are.

Contents

Introduction

Welcome to this self-discovery book and your wonderful journey! Congratulations for being here and seeking to learn more about who you are at your core so you can live fully, shaping your life from within.

I am excited to offer you this book as a guide along your journey toward a deeper, more authentic relationship with yourself. I've been passionate about helping people explore who they are for a very long time. I've been a teacher and a counselor, and I'm a diplomate of the American Institute of Stress. I've written many books, developed course curricula, given presentations and webinars—everything with the purpose of helping people thrive despite challenges big and small.

Personally, I used to live with significant anxiety. I experienced a traumatic brain injury, the effects of which interfered in my life for quite a while. Also, chronic stress and an intrusive sense of toxic perfectionism contributed to my developing several autoimmune and digestive disorders. Initially, I sought useful ways to overcome these obstacles—strategies that I use and have used to help others manage the challenges of life. Along the way, though, I've learned that life is about so much more than overcoming obstacles. The positive and negative things that we experience in life are separate from our deepest, most authentic selves. To be sure, many of our difficulties do involve our own emotions, thoughts, and physical experiences inside our bodies. However, these things don't make up our essence, our real "self." They're merely some of the ways we react to what's happening around us.

What if we could stop reacting to events in our lives and instead begin responding from within, choosing our actions as well as the thoughts we pay attention to and those we let go? What if we began allowing ourselves to accept what we feel in any given moment rather than fighting it or beating ourselves up for it? Imagine for a moment what that might be like. You might find this hard to imagine, because it's so different from what most of us have been taught. We're used to operating according to expectations and demands that may not align with what we want for our lives. You might not even know precisely what it is you want for yourself and your life because you haven't had the opportunity to get to know who you are deep within.

That's where this book comes in! It is your gentle guide and faithful companion as you dive into the process of self-discovery. To discover yourself means to tune out the external noise (the "shoulds," the expectations others may have imposed on you, actions you might have to take that don't quite resonate with you) so you can listen intently to yourself. It also means to settle into yourself comfortably and intimately so your harsh inner critic, the voice that comes from within you but really isn't your own at all, becomes quieter. Then your true voice can finally be heard—by your mind and heart and entire being. You can move through your life with intention and relate to yourself, others, and your tasks with clarity and purpose.

Self-discovery is a gradual process of awakening to all that you are so that you can be with your true self in each moment. That's why this book will travel with you every day for a year (and even longer if you choose to revisit it, because self-discovery is a lifelong adventure). That doesn't mean your journey needs to be overwhelming or arduous. This book consists of daily entries to help you keep the theme of self-discovery on your mind and in your heart each and every day, but the entries are intentionally brief. How you use this book is highly personal, so feel free to experiment to find what works best for you. I offer you these suggestions:

Even though this book starts in January, feel free to start in real time, any day of the year, and progress through it.

Pick a special time, perhaps first thing in the morning, to open it up and read the day's entry.

Let the quotes inspire you as you move through your day.

Repeat the affirmations often to help them sink in.

Allow the reflections to guide you.

Complete the exercises to deepen your experience with the process.

Have a special notebook or journal dedicated to your self-discovery process. You'll find it helpful for the exercises or for recording other inspirations that come to you.

With consistent, daily practice, you can learn a lot about yourself and use the insights you glean to shape your life.

This book can help you work through the roadblocks that keep you from living your life aligned with your best version of yourself. It's not meant to replace professional help, however. I highly encourage you to work with a mental health professional or your doctor if challenges are interfering in your life.

Be lighthearted as you work through this book, and enjoy the process. With the clarity you gain will come the freedom to live more fully in a way that helps you feel vibrant and alive, thriving rather than merely surviving. Get curious, and let's dive into self-discovery!

JANUARY

**My Personality,
My Identity,
My Authentic Self**

———————

1

JANUARY

As you explore your authentic self, the real you underneath any image people might have of you, take care not to label yourself. What is *your* concept of the real you?

2

JANUARY

I am uniquely me and possess varied and valid thoughts, emotions, and values.

3

———

Personality is often conceptualized around what is called the Big Five traits. They exist on a continuum, and we all possess qualities of each to some degree. Without judgment, which words do you think best fit you?

Openness: spontaneous, traditional, habitual, creative, curious, conventional

Conscientiousness: reliable, messy, impulsive, careful, organized, risk-taker

Extraversion: subdued, gregarious, talkative, quiet, reserved, sociable

Agreeableness: critical, forgiving, trusting, indifferent, argumentative, cooperative

Neuroticism: high-strung, anxious, calm, often stressed, laid-back, relaxed

How will you use your traits as you move through your day?

4
JANUARY

How do you allow yourself to be a highly unique mixture of each trait?

5
JANUARY

"I think that personality traits that come through when somebody is really sincere is what makes them beautiful."

—TAYLOR SWIFT

6

From time to time today, pause to sit comfortably, close your eyes, and give yourself a few moments with this centering meditation.

I am becoming open to my experience in each moment as it is.

My own conscientiousness prepares me for my goals.

My level of extraversion serves me in creating the relationships I desire.

When I am agreeable, I work with others for positive outcomes.

When I pause to cultivate calm, I can remain steady in the face of challenge.

7

The Big Five traits influence us, but they don't rigidly determine our hopes and dreams or how we will always respond to life. Contemplate your complexity and spot other traits that make you who you are.

8

JANUARY

Many experts in psychology recognize four personality types that, like the Big Five traits, influence how you perceive your world and shape your actions, thoughts, and feelings. Read these descriptions, then create and describe a unique personality type that fits *you*. Maybe call it Type M for "me."

Type A: Motivated to achieve, driven, perfectionistic

Type B: Creative, even-tempered, laid-back, prone to procrastinate

Type C: Highly conscientious, perfectionistic, and not inclined to showing feelings

Type D: Distressed, anxious, pessimistic, and often withdrawn

9
JANUARY

Consider this as you define yourself: The way we see ourselves is shaped by our memories, but studies show that memories can be positively or negatively biased by our personality traits.

10
JANUARY

Recall a recent or distant memory of yourself and describe it in your notebook. In what ways have you changed since then? In what ways are you the same? As you move forward, what aspects of yourself will you keep, and what no longer serves you?

11
JANUARY

I am not defined by unreliable memories of my past self.

12
JANUARY

The word *personality* comes from the Latin word *persona*, a mask worn by actors to project different roles. Which of your roles do you cherish? Wish to change?

13
JANUARY

Does your personality involve people-pleasing, putting everyone else's needs and interests first? Do you do this out of kindness or fear? What would it be like to honor *your* needs?

14

JANUARY

—

"Tell me what you pay
attention to and I will
tell you who you are."

—JOSÉ ORTEGA Y GASSET

15
JANUARY

Part of our complex personality involves interests—those things that make us want to pay attention and engage. Interests often get lost in life's busyness. Allow yourself now to brainstorm all the things that pique your interest, even if you don't think you could ever do them. Then choose one item on your list and create a plan to do one small thing to add it into your life.

16
JANUARY

Flow, the experience of being challenged and engaged in what you're doing while other thoughts and concerns fade, boosts happiness. Which of your interests put you in a state of flow?

17
JANUARY

Tune in to your musical self. Research has revealed that our personalities influence how we relate to different types of music. Experiment to discover how different types of music influence your emotions, energy levels, and sense of well-being. List different musical genres in your notebook, and then listen to a few new styles. Describe how you respond to each, and then create a growing playlist of "you" music.

18
JANUARY

If you could do anything you wanted with no restrictions, what would you do? What does your answer reveal about you? How can you incorporate a realistic version into your life?

19
JANUARY

Some psychologists divide personality into three parts: "having" personality, "doing" personality, and "being" personality.

You have a personality. Describe aspects of your nature that make you *you*.

Your personality is constantly in motion. What goals and actions are an important part of who you are?

You belong to a bigger picture and are part of a story full of plot twists and turning points. What outside influences have shaped you?

20
JANUARY

In addition to personality, you have an identity, made up of your unique set of beliefs, values, abilities, behaviors, and relationships. How do you describe yourself to others?

21

Describe yourself in the context of these aspects of identity. Where do you fit? Would you shift anything? Why or why not?

Abilities:

Age:

Family:

Culture:

Ethnicity:

Gender:

Religion:

Sexual orientation:

Socioeconomic status:

22

JANUARY

Mindfulness involves living fully in each moment of your life instead of living on autopilot or stuck in feelings about what is happening, what already happened, or what might happen in the future. Mindfulness enriches our lives in many ways, including our relationship with ourselves and our identity. As you move through your day, pay attention mindfully to how facets of your identity influence your thoughts, feelings, and actions. Are there ways you might draw on them more intentionally to feel more fulfilled?

23

JANUARY

I am proud of my rich and varied self.

24
JANUARY

Your identity is both a mountain and a river. It forms a solid foundation of who you are, yet it is constantly flowing, shifting, and changing as you grow. Which aspects of yourself feel most steady? Which feel most malleable?

25
JANUARY

Sketch a mountain and a river. On the mountain, draw symbols or write words that depict or describe the aspects of you that feel most steady. These are concepts that resonate with you deeply and feel like you at your very core. You wouldn't be "you" without them. On the river, draw or write descriptions of parts of yourself that feel less permanent.

26
JANUARY

___

Study the river you drew with its depiction of your changing identity.

List some goals you have for personal growth in these areas.

For each goal, list one action step to move toward it.

Circle one goal, and commit to implementing the action step today.

27
JANUARY

___

An identity crisis can happen when something challenges your sense of self. The stronger your sense of who you are, the steadier your thoughts, feelings, and actions will be in the face of personal challenge. In your notebook, write about what you have learned about yourself so far.

28

Self-determination refers to making choices and engaging in behaviors that align with your unique identity and personality. Let this meditation guide you in living with self-determination.

As I inhale, I breathe in the essence of who I am.

As I hold my breath, I let my essence flow throughout my being.

As I exhale, I breathe out purpose, peace, and confidence in myself.

29
JANUARY

While being our authentic self is crucial, we also
need to function in relationships. How can you
find a balance between honoring yourself while
also allowing others to honor themselves?

30
JANUARY

—

Think about a challenge you're facing, perhaps in a relationship or at work. Now think about the identity you made for yourself on January 24 and 25 (page 16). How can you use those tools to help you face this challenge and move past it?

31
JANUARY

—

"I don't cover my face because I want to show my identity."

—MALALA YOUSAFZAI

FEBRUARY

Lovingkindness for Myself and in My Life

———————

1

FEBRUARY

Self-acceptance is tied to well-being, but it can be difficult. What makes it hard for you to accept and love yourself?

2

FEBRUARY

Embrace yourself completely. Accept your humanity with all your positives and negatives. Observe yourself today without judgment. Simply pay attention to your thoughts, feelings, and actions as if you were watching a movie. When you catch yourself evaluating with criticism, gently remember, "Whoops. Judging." Then shift your attention back to neutral and observe yourself being wonderfully you.

3

FEBRUARY

Catch the good in your thoughts, feelings, and actions today, and celebrate in the moment. Do a little dance, savor the taste of something you enjoy, or high-five yourself.

4

FEBRUARY

Describe your body from the perspective of someone head over heels in love with you. What beauty do they see? Write your description with as much detail as possible. What does this person see in your face, movements, size, shape, and actions? Remember that this person loves you fully for all that you are, and they don't want to change you.

5

FEBRUARY

Write a letter of gratitude to your body and physical health. Write about any limitations (illness, pain, mobility restrictions, etc.) with an attitude of tenderness and understanding. Acknowledge with thankfulness all that you can do and the parts of you that feel well.

6

FEBRUARY

"To love oneself is the beginning of a lifelong romance."

—OSCAR WILDE

The childhood chant
"Sticks and stones may break my bones,
but words will never hurt me"
is untrue. Your words of self-criticism
hurt. Develop the habit of catching
and rephrasing your harsh words.

8

FEBRUARY

Lovingkindness meditations help us be gentle with ourselves. It helps to repeat the wishes we direct toward ourselves often so they can gradually sink in. As they do, we come to look upon ourselves with the tenderness of someone who cares. We realize that we deserve these positive outcomes. Lovingkindness takes time to internalize, so use this traditional meditation regularly.

May I be healthy.

May I be secure.

May I be joyful.

May I live with ease.

9

FEBRUARY

Healthy perfectionism can help us achieve our goals, whereas toxic perfectionism causes incredible stress and is damaging to mental and physical health. What is your relationship with perfectionism?

10

FEBRUARY

Toxic perfectionism on one hand and lack of focused discipline on the other both threaten our safety and well-being from within, keeping us stressed and anxious. What would it be like for you to seek a middle ground of "good enough?"

11

FEBRUARY

I am valuable for who I am, not for what I do.

12
FEBRUARY
—

Metaphorically, dance in the **RAIN** to develop self-compassion and lovingkindness with a mindfulness exercise originally from Michele McDonald and later adapted by Tara Brach.

Recognize your self-critical thoughts and feelings.

Allow them to be there, accepting their presence but distancing yourself from their content.

Investigate with curiosity rather than harsh self-judgment. What is happening right now that contributes to these thoughts and feelings?

Natural awareness comes from mindfulness. Pull yourself out of your thoughts and feelings and center yourself in your present moment.

13
FEBRUARY

Begin to separate yourself from your harsh inner critic. That critical voice may be inside you, but it isn't *you*. It's likely a conglomeration of people and messages from the past that continue to influence you in the present. List some perfectionistic thoughts. Take a step back from them by reminding yourself that these are only thoughts, and they don't accurately represent reality. Rewrite them to be more realistic.

14
FEBRUARY

Self-compassion isn't fluff. Studies show that it reduces stress, anxiety, depression, and other difficulties. Take five minutes every day to offer yourself words of kindness and encouragement.

15

FEBRUARY

Many of us seek acceptance and approval from other people, but this undermines our own self-acceptance. How much of your self-concept is based on others' opinions of you?

16

FEBRUARY

Think about expectations others have had for you. Allow yourself to consider how much of this resonates with you and what you'd like to let go of or embrace.

17

FEBRUARY

How often do you do things you don't want to do in order to please others or win their approval? Are you engaging in a healthy compromise of give-and-take, or are you often sacrificing yourself to avoid conflict or disapproval? Ponder the effects that approval-seeking or people-pleasing have on your life and well-being. Describe what it would be like for you to begin to do what feels right for *you*.

18

FEBRUARY

To do what feels right for you, you first must know yourself. Contemplate what your heart wants in your relationships and what goals are on your mind.

19
FEBRUARY

I choose to treat myself with patience and kindness.

20
FEBRUARY

Think of well-being and self-compassion as four "A's": awareness, acceptance, attention, and action.

Become aware of how you talk to yourself and how your whole being listens.

Practice deep self-acceptance. Accept your mistakes and your triumphs.

Choose what you pay attention to. Rather than ruminating about blunders, rehashing the past, or predicting failure, pay attention to yourself as you truly are in each moment.

Decide which purposeful actions you want to take that feel right for you.

21

FEBRUARY

I gently forgive myself for my mistakes.

22

FEBRUARY

Negative emotions are part of the human experience. The next time you experience a negative emotion (hate, anger, frustration), sit with it for a minute. Rather than push it away, show yourself some tenderness and offer a word of encouragement.

23
FEBRUARY

We often criticize ourselves harshly, thinking that we must always push ourselves to be better. However, this is more hurtful than helpful and keeps us stuck. In your notebook, list some of your self-criticisms ("I'm ridiculous." "I always mess things up." "I'm a bad parent/spouse/friend/etc."). Now revisit that list and make your statements more accurate and kinder. For example, "I always mess things up" might become "I made a mistake this morning, and I took a specific action afterward to move forward."

24
FEBRUARY
—

Feelings of guilt and remorse over the past prevent us from living fully in the present and make self-acceptance seem out of reach. What would self-forgiveness be like for you?

25

FEBRUARY

———

If you're having a hard time forgiving yourself for something in your past, try this exercise for letting go and releasing yourself. Reflect on what happened and who was involved. What can you do now, in the present, to move past it? Do you need to apologize or do something to make amends? Do what you can, and accept what you can't. Consider what lesson you've learned about yourself, and allow yourself to refocus on the present and the future.

26

FEBRUARY

———

Sometimes we feel shame or guilt for things beyond our control. If you are stuck on a problem for which you weren't responsible, journal about the situation. Describe what transpired as well as your thoughts and feelings about it. Reread it, and consider it from the point of view of someone neutral who is merely observing. With this distance between you and your memory, rewrite the situation with less judgment and more kindness toward yourself.

27
FEBRUARY

I let go of my past self and celebrate who I am today.

28
FEBRUARY

Plan a special day to simply be with yourself. This is a day to celebrate yourself, all that you are, and the growth and changes you are intentionally engaging in. Begin by accepting that you deserve this time. Then decide how you want to cherish yourself. How will you express your lovingkindness? How will you treat yourself? Commit to a day and schedule it on the calendar with resolve.

29

FEBRUARY

—

"If you could
only sense how
important you
are to the
lives of those
you meet."

—FRED ROGERS

40

MARCH

My Purpose and Meaning

1
MARCH

Meaning exists in moments, one at a time.

2
MARCH

Living with purpose means knowing what is important to you and letting that guide your actions. Your life with purpose is a highly personal adventure. It's not necessary to take grand, sweeping actions to change the world. Purpose can be quiet and subtle. Meaning is what matters to you.

"You are your best thing."

—TONI MORRISON

4
MARCH

Research has shown that discovering and cultivating a sense of meaning and purpose reduces anxiety and depression. Journal about a challenging situation. How might the goals and values that steer you help you deal positively with this situation? Living with meaning won't magically eradicate an obstacle, but it does have the power to change your perspective.

5
MARCH

Be mindfully meaningful. Notice this moment and consider what small things you can do right now to make it matter.

6
MARCH

Go on a mindful scavenger hunt to explore your sense of meaning. Walk around your home or take a walk outside. Identify sights, scents, and textures that you find particularly pleasing. Get curious, and explore why you delight in them. Do they evoke fond memories? Do they remind you of activities you love? Consider how you can re-create these experiences on purpose.

7
MARCH

I make decisions based on what is meaningful to me.

8

MARCH

Pause to embrace the silence, and create space inside of you for a sense of meaning to develop.

Light a candle, and sit or stand comfortably in front of it.

Observe its light, its flickering flame, as you breathe slowly and deeply.

Visualize its warm glow entering your body with every inhale.

Hold the inhale, and imagine the light filling your entire being, illuminating your deepest desires.

Exhale, and feel light and energized to live with purpose.

9
MARCH

Know this: As long as you are not intentionally bringing harm to yourself or others, there is absolutely no wrong meaning, and no incorrect sense of purpose in life.

10
MARCH

Allow yourself to let go of rules and expectations, including what you think you "should" find meaningful. As you reflect on your unique reasons for doing what you do, listen to your inner voice. When exploring what is meaningful to you, ask yourself where it is coming from. If it feels like an imposition from someone else, give yourself permission to trade it in for something closer to your own heart.

11
MARCH

"He who has a why to live for can
bear almost any how."

—FRIEDRICH NIETZSCHE

12
MARCH

Your freedom to be fully you comes from your unique sense of
purpose. What are you living for today?

13

During the Nazi regime, psychiatrist Viktor Frankl spent a grueling four years in Hitler's concentration camps, including the death camps Auschwitz and Dachau. During the Holocaust, he lost his entire family and witnessed unspeakable horrors. Yet he observed that not everyone was broken by these atrocities. Those who found meaning in their experiences and used it to guide their days and nights transcended their suffering to survive with strength. After the war, he used this insight to create logotherapy, a mental health approach that helps people create their own meaning in their lives. What personal sense of meaning helps you thrive despite your own hardships?

14
MARCH

Having a clear life map to guide us can help us live intentionally. It reveals your reasons for doing what you do (your *why*), and it helps you plan action steps for your path forward (your *how*). In your notebook, reflect on a specific goal. Why is this goal important to you—what greater meaning does it hold? How can you incorporate this meaning into your life today, even if you haven't quite reached it?

15
MARCH

What actions and words will create deeper, more meaningful interactions today with the people closest to you, acquaintances, and strangers in passing?

16
MARCH

Think of a challenge you're facing and how you can approach it with openness. Rather than judging it negatively, resisting, reacting emotionally, or avoiding, instead reflect on how facing this challenge will help you grow. What meaning can you identify in it, even if that sense of meaning is simple and small? What will this say about who you are? Write about this in your notebook.

17
MARCH

Purpose is a work in progress. Open your mind and heart to what makes you feel alive, and don't close the door. Continually ask yourself, "What feels right for me now?"

18
MARCH

Recall a time when you felt proud of yourself. What was it that brought you this sense of self-satisfaction? How can you do more of it?

19
MARCH

Create a collage to help you identify what is meaningful to you. Find images and inspirational words or phrases, cut them out, and paste them in a special notebook or on a large sheet of poster board. Alternatively, you can create an electronic collage if you love working with technology. This can become a vision board that reminds you of your own uniquely wonderful *why*.

20

MARCH

Slow down and allow yourself to enjoy exploring your personal meaning. There is no pressure of time to develop your sense of meaning.

21

MARCH

It can be difficult to live with purpose and intention when we're depleted. Carve out some time today to replenish yourself. When you rest and relax, you give your body and mind a chance to de-stress. Yoga, meditating, reading an enjoyable book, or simply engaging in a fun hobby are all rejuvenating. Notice how resetting regularly gradually renews your sense of vitality and purpose.

22
MARCH

—

"The mystery of human existence
lies not in just staying alive, but in
finding something to live for."

—FYODOR DOSTOYEVSKY

23
MARCH

—

When we keep our sense of purpose at the forefront of our mind, we expand how we interpret people, situations, and experiences. Challenge yourself to look beyond the ordinary and find meaning in small things. Use your notebook to record your experiences with going deeper in this way. How does it affect how you see yourself?

24
MARCH

How do you already feel fulfilled in your life? Perhaps you feel deep satisfaction with your family, work, or a hobby. How would your sense of meaning deepen by expanding these experiences to make them more prominent in your life?

25
MARCH

Contemplate your culture. What are some shared values and beliefs that shed light on what "meaning" and "purpose" signify in the context of your heritage? To what degree do they fit with your own? List some key principles, and use them to shape a meaningful goal.

26
MARCH

Many of our problems are signals that we've veered off track from our sense of purpose. When something doesn't resonate with you, listen to what it's telling your deepest self.

27
MARCH

Identify your purpose in each situation. Instead of avoiding problems, accept that they exist and respond in ways that align with your vision of yourself.

28
MARCH

We can't always choose what happens to us, but we can choose our response. Instead of instantly reacting to difficult people and situations, pause first. Take a deep breath. Ask yourself, "What outcome do I want? What can I do or say right now, with intent, to move toward a more meaningful resolution?"

29
MARCH

Meaning can be found in the most basic experiences. How have you imbued your living space with personal meaning?

30
MARCH

Make meaningful meals. Mealtime is a moment for nourishing your body and mind. Pick one meal this week and dedicate it to slowing down. Choose food that you enjoy, perhaps a cherished comfort food that evokes fond memories. Prepare it with intention, paying attention to the whole process. Sit comfortably and eat mindfully, with no distractions. Eat slowly, relishing the sight, smell, texture, and taste. Find meaning in this experience.

31
MARCH

I choose to create a meaningful life,

one moment at a time.

APRIL

Discovering My Resilience

1
APRIL

"You may not control
all the events that happened
to you, but you can decide
not to be reduced by them."

—MAYA ANGELOU

2

APRIL

You can fall. You can fail. You can react badly sometimes. You can make all sorts of mistakes. Being resilient doesn't mean you'll never do these things. It means messing up and then getting back up, dusting yourself off, and choosing how you want to progress. Knowing your purpose, the spark that drives your goal, helps with resilience. In your notebook, describe why you keep going in the face of obstacles. What inner resources help you do it?

3

APRIL

Resilience has less to do with talent and intelligence and more to do with attitude and effort. How much effort are you willing to expend to overcome an obstacle you're facing?

4
APRIL

Bouncing back from a difficulty or dealing with stress can sometimes mean leaving a problem in the past and focusing on
the present and future. What are you looking forward to today?

5
APRIL

When we're stressed, we automatically breathe more rapidly and shallowly.
Changing how you breathe when facing challenges impacts the actions you
take and how quickly you bounce back. Inhale slowly and deeply, noticing
where in your body you feel your breath the strongest. Maybe it's the air entering your nostrils, your chest expanding, or your belly rising. That is your anchor
point. Concentrate on that spot as you take several slow, deep breaths. The
next time you are feeling stressed, use anchor breathing to stabilize yourself.

6

APRIL

I meet my obstacles with calm and grace.

7

APRIL

Recall a setback you recently faced. It could be big or small. Write down your immediate thoughts and emotions about it. In light of your evidence, put your setback in perspective. How can you grow from it?

8
APRIL

A traditional Japanese saying calls to us, "Fall seven, rise eight."
What motivates you to rise again and again?

9
APRIL

How we talk to ourselves affects how quickly we can recover from setbacks. In
your notebook, make a list of unhelpful things you say to yourself. For example,
do you say things like "I'm so stupid" or "I always ruin everything"? Rewrite each
statement to help you start changing your self-talk. For example, "I don't know
everything, but I'm intelligent" or "I enhance lives because I _____."

10
APRIL

Did you know that it's our feelings that start the fight–flight–or–freeze reaction when we face stress? Tune in to your emotions. By building awareness, you can decide how to address your feelings to combat stress and build resiliency.

11
APRIL

We can't always choose what happens to us, but we can always choose our response.

12
APRIL

Our thoughts about problems pull us out of the present moment and prevent us from bouncing back and moving forward. Use this mindfulness exercise to center yourself and deal with stressful situations: Think of someone who reminds you of why resilience matters to you. Focus your attention on this person, mentally noting as many details as you can. What would they do in a similar situation? Let them inspire you now.

13
APRIL

What would it be like to embrace failure as a chance to tap into your strengths differently and try again? How would it change how you view yourself?

14
APRIL

"A hero is an ordinary individual who
finds the strength to persevere and endure
in spite of overwhelming obstacles."
—CHRISTOPHER REEVE

15
APRIL

Well-being isn't the absence of stress, problems, conflict, or loss. Well-being is responding to these obstacles with resolve to keep going. Today, catch your resolve to persevere, and celebrate it.

16

APRIL

A gatha is a short, meditative verse that helps us be present in whatever is happening right now. Use this gatha to help you pause and reset in a moment of stress. Repeat it once, or several times, to help you center and focus. Then continue what you were doing with an attitude of strength and resiliency.

Breathing in, I am calm.

Breathing out, I know I have choices.

I respond positively to this challenge.

I am centered and strong.

17
APRIL

Resilience isn't something we're born with. It's not something for which we have a limited capacity. Even if bouncing back from stress, adversity, challenge, and loss has always been difficult, you aren't doomed to be forever vulnerable to setbacks. Resiliency is a skill, an outlook, an approach to responding to challenge, and it is never too late to start building it. Call to mind someone you respect and admire, and imagine them facing a setback. Which of their qualities do you already possess, and which would you like to develop?

18
APRIL

Real-time resilience refers to positively dealing with problems in the moment they are happening. When you face stress today, pause, breathe deeply, and choose your action intentionally.

19
APRIL

Resilience comes from within us, and it can also come from outside us: from the support systems and resources in our lives. Make a list of people you can rely on to help you through tough times. What about resources available in your community? Do you have a library to seek knowledge? Do you have local support groups? Think of what you need, and explore how your community can provide it.

20
APRIL

Even during difficult times, in each moment, you have the power to choose your attitude and your actions. Catch yourself feeling helpless. What new thought or action would be helpful?

21

APRIL

Hardiness is a trait associated with resilience. People who are hardy find meaning in life's ups and downs and embrace challenge as opportunities to grow. Write a story or account of a recent setback you faced. In what ways did it trip you up? Rewrite that story as if it were a gift, an opportunity to make a positive change or use your skills in new ways. In this new version, what meaning do you discover in the experience? What have you learned about yourself?

22

APRIL

We are more resilient when we believe that our actions matter in any given situation. As you move through your day, be aware of all the ways your actions matter.

23
APRIL

When have you shown resilience, and how were you able to keep going? What aspects of your resiliency are you proud of? In what ways would you like to grow?

24
APRIL

Stress, hardship, loss, and adversity can skew our perspective, making everything dull and negative. This can be defeating and depleting, robbing us of the energy we need to take positive action. Re-energize by developing mindful awareness of all the positive aspects in your present moment, no matter how small. Go on a photo safari, taking pictures of things little and big that make you smile, inspire wonder, give you hope for the future, or make you feel motivated.

25
APRIL

—

"As Duckworth has said, 'I learned a lesson I'd never forget. The lesson was that, when you have setbacks and failures, you can't overreact to them.'"

—SHERYL SANDBERG AND ADAM M. GRANT

26
APRIL

—

Talking about mistakes has a way of shrinking them. It can be anxiety-provoking and uncomfortable telling someone about something you did wrong, but doing so can help you process it and find new solutions. Who do you feel safe talking to about a failure or setback? Invite them for coffee or tea, and ask them to help you problem-solve. Afterward, reflect on what you learned about yourself and how the conversation contributed to your growth.

27
APRIL

Carry this gentle reminder with you: Most problems are neither pervasive nor permanent. Identify what's going well now and what you're looking forward to.

28
APRIL

Hope is an important part of resilience. It's the expectation that problems won't last. Do you resolve to make today better than yesterday?

29
APRIL

Do you tend to blame yourself for problems and difficult situations? Transform feelings of guilt and self-blame by broadening your perspective. Was a set-back or failure completely your fault? List the things that contributed to the situation, and circle all the things that were beyond your control. Of the things that were in your control, identify what you did right and be proud of them. Consider your mistakes, and rather than berate yourself, identify how you will make changes going forward.

30
APRIL

I have the inner strength I need to begin again.

MAY

Discovering My Work, Paid or Unpaid

———

1
MAY

"Work" and "career" refer to so much more than paid employment. Whether or not you have a paid job, you do work and have a career, because these terms apply to the whole of what you do in your life. Write your own career description, one that reflects your completeness and honors all that you do in your days. Then summarize the essence of your work in two sentences: "I am _____." I do _____."

2
MAY

"Doing what you love is the cornerstone of having abundance in your life."

—WAYNE DYER

3

MAY

In what ways do you bring yourself—your personality, abilities, interests, ambitions, and values—to all the various tasks you do every day?

4

MAY

Even if you're not actively seeking new employment, writing a résumé or a letter of introduction can help you discover and appreciate new aspects of yourself that you might otherwise discount or take for granted. Imagine that you are applying for the job of your dreams (even if you already are living it), and create a résumé or write a letter showcasing all you have to offer.

5
MAY

Doing work we're interested in is linked to life satisfaction and career success. Today, pay attention to how your own work aligns with your interests.

6
MAY

Our jobs aren't always exciting. However, there are things you can do to spice up your work and infuse it with elements that help you stay engaged. For one week, as you work and complete the duties of your job, think about what you like to do. Write down what you enjoy the most about your job and the areas in which you excel. Keep this list for future exercises about self-discovery and work.

7
MAY

At least half of our waking hours are spent working. That's a big chunk of our lives. How does your work affect your thoughts, emotions, and energy for your other hours?

8
MAY

I actively identify the positives in my work experiences.

9
MAY

Beginning your day with a cherished ritual prepares you to respond calmly to work challenges. Consider awakening 10 minutes earlier to meditate, stretch, or enjoy a quiet cup of coffee or tea.

10
MAY

Sally Maitlis of Oxford University exhorts, "If you love what you do, then small problems that come up aren't going to bug you and make you want to quit. But when you love it to the point that it's absolutely central to how you understand yourself and what your contribution to the world is, it can be damaging." In your notebook, reflect on the qualities you have, independent of your work identity, that contribute to the world.

11
MAY

Sometimes we endure a job because it allows us to enjoy other aspects of our lives. What drives your perseverance? Why do you keep doing what you do?

12
MAY

Take your list of what you enjoy most about your work and the areas you excel, and look for jobs or volunteer positions with those key phrases. Identify at least three to five opportunities where your skills would be a good fit.

13
MAY
—

"Success is liking yourself, liking what
you do, and liking how you do it."
—MAYA ANGELOU

14
MAY
—

Feeling a sense of connection and belonging in your daily work is
an important part of satisfaction and contentment. Notice all the
little and big ways you fit where you are.

15
MAY

It's easy to get caught up in the stress and demands of our work. When that happens, we risk losing sight of ourselves. Carve out time today to pause and reflect on all that you have achieved, successes big and small, in your work life. Celebrate how far you have come by doing one thing you love today, perhaps sitting and listening to your favorite song, making your favorite food for dinner, or enjoying time in nature.

16
MAY

What aspects of your work do you love? The mission, people, the use of your strengths and talents, your personal meaning? Intentionally focus on the part(s) of your work that make your heart sing.

17
MAY

What work tasks have you been so engrossed in that you lost track of time? Can you seek opportunities to be involved in more tasks like this?

18

MAY

We all face limitations that can frustrate us and impede our progress toward our career goals. Limitations can come from within us, such as abilities, beliefs, and perspectives. Limitations can also be external, for example, specific circumstances or people we work with. Journal about a limitation that is getting in your way. Use it to create a new work goal, and list the steps you need to get started. What abilities, strengths, and talents will you use?

19

MAY

---

*My work
helps
me grow in
new ways
every day.*

20

MAY

A nightly meditation practice can help you close your day positively. You might sit comfortably to help you remain awake during this meditation or lie in bed, allowing it to guide you to sleep.

Today, I did my best.

My best varies from day to day, and that is okay.

My heart is content with _____.

My mind is proud of _____.

My body served me well, and I took care of it.

Today is done.

Tomorrow is full of promise.

21

MAY

If you could make any changes to your work life, what would they be? Why? Why not start today, with one small goal and one small action step.

22

MAY

Approaching the various realms of your day mindfully, rather than trying to multitask, can be fulfilling. Center yourself in the moment by identifying your role and purpose. Consider how you want to be and what you want to do. Give the task (or person) at hand your full attention. Remove all distractions, including your phone, and engage completely. Try this with just one task today, and gradually approach more of your tasks and roles with mindful engagement.

23
MAY
—

What fears or worries are blocking your ability to enjoy your work?
To help loosen their grip, identify one thing that will move you a
little further away from them.

24
MAY
—

"Work gives you meaning and purpose,
and life is empty without it."

—STEPHEN HAWKING

25
MAY

Spending long periods of time sitting has been found to negatively affect both physical and mental health. If your work involves quite a bit of sitting, try setting a timer to sound every hour. When it sounds, take a break to move in a way that honors your body. You might do some gentle stretches, take a brief mindful walk, or even just turn your head to look at something fresh while you wiggle your fingers.

26
MAY

What roles do you play in your life, and which are most important to you? Do you spend enough time in that role to satisfy yourself?

27
MAY

I contribute to my world in
meaningful ways every day.

28
MAY

Volunteering can help us pursue our passions and live with meaning. In what ways could you offer your enthusiasm and energy to something important to you?

29

MAY

Pursue professional growth. What would help you do more of what you do well? Make a list of activities that will help you advance, such as taking a class or attending a webinar, networking, joining a relevant group, or connecting with a mentor. Identify why you'd like to do this and what you might gain. Then commit to doing it and create a plan for your growth.

30

MAY

What does success mean to you and in your life? You might reflect on finances, relationships, freedom, passions, purpose, opportunities to use your skills, and more.

31

MAY

Pausing between tasks can reduce stress and allow you to mentally shift gears. Use this breathing exercise to transition.

Select something that has a pleasing scent, such as a candle or a drop of oil. Alternatively, step outside and take in the smell of fresh air.

Close your eyes and inhale deeply, noticing and appreciating the scent.

Imagine the scent traveling through your body and mind, both invigorating and calming you.

Exhale completely.

JUNE

Discovering Myself in My Relationships and Community

1
JUNE

My relationships enhance rather
than define who I am.

2
JUNE

Celebrating little things with someone deepens connections and enhances self-esteem. Identify something positive in your day, and share it with someone. Celebrate with a high five, special meal, or walk together. How does this differ from those times when you ignored the positives, either focusing instead on talking about the negatives, or kept the positives to yourself without celebrating them?

3
JUNE

In the field of positive psychology, other people are key to our well-being. To what extent are other people a component of your happiness?

4
JUNE

As you move through your day, take time to connect more deeply with at least one person. What new insights do you gain about yourself in doing this?

5
JUNE

___

What would it be like for you to be intentional about creating and working toward clear relationship goals? Use the SMART technique to be intentional about a relationship goal. Think of one goal, and elaborate on it to make it *Specific, Measurable, Attainable, Relevant, and Time-based.* For example, *I will communicate my needs in the moment by calmly telling my partner that today I'd enjoy having a quiet evening at home.*

6
JUNE

"You'll never be able to find yourself if you're lost in someone else."

—COLLEEN HOOVER, *NOVEMBER 9*

7
JUNE

We all make sacrifices for relationships, but this doesn't mean abandoning what is important to us. What do you like about yourself that you don't want to give up for a relationship?

8
JUNE

For Harvard psychiatrist George Vaillant, a researcher who has linked positive social connections to longevity, the most important human strength is the ability to be loved. Many of us, though, find it difficult to accept love. Start a running list of all of the many reasons you are worthy of love. I'll start you off: You are worthy of love because you are uniquely, wonderfully you. Now it's your turn to uncover your unique and wonderful, love-worthy qualities.

9
JUNE

How rushed are you in your interactions with loved ones? What would it be like to slow down in one specific area? What about in a daily routine?

10
JUNE

Practice mindful listening in your relationships. This involves actively connecting with someone when they talk to you, giving them your undivided attention, and focusing on what they're saying rather than remaining lost in your own thoughts. Concentrate on the person you're with—their words, tone, facial expressions, and posture—to stay grounded in the moment. Reflect in your journal about how mindful listening helps deepen your relationships.

11
JUNE

I accept myself and others.

12
JUNE

Expressing gratitude for others has been found to strengthen relationships and positively impact not just for the person receiving the gratitude but also for the person expressing it. Write a letter of gratitude to someone, thanking them for something specific they did for you and how it has affected your life. How are you a better person because of this person's influence? Send them the letter, or even better, read it to them in person.

13
JUNE

How do you share yourself with your loved ones, coworkers, or your greater community? How do these people help you grow?

14
JUNE

"Strong communities are born out of individuals being their best selves."

—LEANNE BETASAMOSAKE SIMPSON

15
JUNE

Human connection is an important part of life for introverts and extroverts alike. In what ways, big or small, do belong in your community?

16
JUNE

What are your limits on what you will tolerate in relationships? What types of behavior and words are okay with you, and what isn't?

17

JUNE

Emotions, either suppressing them or impulsively reacting to them, can interfere in relationships. Use this meditation to develop a healthy relationship with your emotions and use them to guide you rather than impede you in your interactions.

As you breathe slowly and deeply, begin to notice your emotions in your mind and body.

Sit with them, breathing and noticing. Don't try to change them.

Name an emotion without judging it. "I feel _____."

Return your attention to your breath, relaxing with every exhale.

When you feel centered, you can calmly decide what action, if any, you want to take to address the feeling.

18
JUNE

I grow stronger in my relationships every day.

19
JUNE

Make and eat a mindful meal with someone in your life. Invite someone to plan, shop for, and prepare a special meal with you. Together, set the table and even decorate it as if it were a special occasion (it is!). Remove distractions such as smartphones and the television. Reflect on the experience afterward. How difficult was it to be completely engaged in this activity with this person? What would it be like to have mindful meals together more often?

20
JUNE

Having healthy boundaries in relationships helps you preserve your sense of identity. How do you balance time spent with and without your partner?

21
JUNE

Performing acts of kindness is more than just fluff for social media posts. Numerous studies have found that active kindness increases well-being. Do your own experiment. Go out of your way this week to perform small acts of kindness for loved ones and strangers. Record your deeds in your journal, and reflect on how each one affected your mood and feelings about yourself.

22
JUNE

Is there a difference between your idea of the "real" you and the one you present to others?

23
JUNE

What would it be like to share your vulnerabilities with someone close to you? What do you fear might happen? How might trusting yourself and others enrich your life?

24
JUNE

—

"The greatest obstacle to love is the hidden fear of not being worthy of being loved."

—SPANISH PROVERB

25
JUNE

—

Use this gatha to help you honor your authentic self in relationships.

Breathing in, I know that I am worthy of love.

Breathing out, I know that I have love to give.

I confidently remain true to my values, beliefs, and interests.

I allow others to explore their values, beliefs, and interests, too.

26

JUNE

Sketch a mountain range with multiple peaks. Think about people in your life and write their names (or draw and label them) on various peaks, one person per peak. Now think about what you have in common with each of them, including personality traits, shared values, common interests, etc. Write these on each peak. Reflect on which peaks you'd like to spend more of your time. Create an intention to connect more deeply with specific people.

27

JUNE

Try an experiment today. Strike up a conversation with someone new, perhaps someone who seems lonely or isolated. Notice how it makes you feel about yourself.

28
JUNE
—

Discover more about your place in your world. On a blank sheet of paper, draw a circle with two rings around it. Write "ME" in the center circle. In the next ring, write names of family members, coworkers or classmates, neighbors, and other close acquaintances. In the following ring, list community centers, organizations, institutions, and other places you interact with. Describe the positive interactions you have with the people and systems in your life. What would you like to change?

29
JUNE

People show love and appreciation in many different ways. Watch for all the different ways the people in your life show care and respect for you.

30
JUNE

I value who I am and what I bring to my relationships.

JULY

**Discovering My Passions
and Interests**

"Don't ask yourself what the world needs. Ask yourself what makes you come alive, and go do that, because what the world needs is people who have come alive."

—HOWARD THURMAN

2
JULY

What makes you feel most alive? Identify this heart of your passions, and commit to actively pursuing these things at least once per week.

3
JULY

Dedicate some time and attention to discovering new interests. Schedule a trip to your local library or bookstore, and browse sections that are new to you. Wander the aisles, pull random books from the shelves, and thumb through them. Notice what grabs your attention, and check out or purchase a few books on the topic. As you discover new interests, identify ways you can actively make them part of your life.

4

JULY

———

Sometimes discovering interests and passions in the ordinary and mundane stuff of our lives can add greater depth to the daily grind. Intentionally finding things to be interested in can bring its own excitement. As you move through your day, pretend that you're new to each activity and find things that fascinate you. Notice what you learn about yourself in the process.

5

JULY

———

Do you prefer pursuing more individual interests (things you do on your own) or social interests (doing things with groups)? How might you grow if you explored the opposite?

6
JULY

I spice up my days by searching for interesting people, situations, and activities.

7
JULY

What was (or is) your favorite school subject? What did you enjoy about it? How would pursuing that topic in a new way lead to personal development?

8

JULY

Life is busy, and it can be difficult to find the time and energy needed to pursue our passions and interests. To get around this, discover how exactly you are spending your time. For a few days, pay attention to what you do, jotting down your activities in your notebook. Then study it honestly. Are there things you habitually do, such as collapsing in front of the TV in the evening, that you could replace with something you find more exciting and fulfilling, something that aligns with your interests?

9
JULY

Devote time today to an interesting activity, and pay close attention to how it impacts your thoughts, emotions, energy, and general mood.

10
JULY

According to positive psychologists, interests are more than what we do. They're integral to our inner selves, and part of our individual traits. Today, notice what intrigues you and what that says about you.

11
JULY
—

Personality and interests are closely related. You can use categories developed by psychologist John Holland to learn more about yourself and discover what types of work and play you find interesting. Which of these descriptions resonate most strongly with you? (You can pick multiple categories.)

Artistic: taking pleasure in creating (any form)

Conventional: enjoying working with data, keeping records

Enterprising: oriented toward workplace goals and economic gain

Investigative: interested in observing and studying concepts

Realistic: enjoying manipulating objects, tools, machines

Social: preferring doing things with others

12
JULY

"A hobby a day keeps the doldrums away."
—PHYLLIS MCGINLEY

13
JULY

When we consider interests, we often automatically think of activities. In reality, we're intrigued by so much more, including people. Who interests you? Maybe you think of people you know, complete strangers, or even historical figures. What is it about these people that fascinates you? What does this tell you about who you are? Write about this in your notebook, focusing on what your interest in others teaches you about yourself.

14
JULY

Engaging in interesting activities is linked to positive emotions like joy and contentment. Today, note how doing different things affects your mood.

15
JULY

Look through old photo albums or scrapbooks. Notice your emotions as you do, and linger over things that arouse feelings of excitement or joy. What is happening in those memories? What insights about yourself and your interests do they awaken? Identify at least one way you can use these insights to reignite these feelings and passions in your current life.

16
JULY

A big part of feeling passionate about what you're doing is savoring it. Whenever you're engaging in an activity you find interesting, pay attention to it fully and remove distractions like your phone.

17
JULY

I increase my energy and motivation by exploring my interests.

18
JULY

Activities that put us in a state of flow, in which
we're fully engaged in what we're doing, are challenging but not overly difficult. What activities
do you find to be most balanced between boring
and frustrating?

19
JULY

It can be helpful to think of interests as things you find fun and passions as things that you care deeply about. While there is, of course, much overlap between the two, thinking about these concepts separately can help you learn about what drives you. Recall the exercise on July 3 (page 125) in which you browsed through a library or bookstore. Take what you discovered and categorize topics into lists representing "What I find fun" and "What I care about." Which list creates the most positive emotion?

20
JULY

To what extent do you get to do interesting things in your work or at play every day? Honestly reflecting on this can help you learn more about yourself and approach each day with greater intention.

21
JULY

Why do certain activities or topics excite you? (Do you feel competent? Enthusiastic? Relaxed? Validated? Something else?) What insights about yourself do you gain when you explore the answer to this question?

22
JULY

According to positive psychologists, the amount of time we devote to pursuing our interests in our leisure time directly correlates to how satisfied we feel with our lives. For one week, track your time to discover new insights about how you're spending it. Every day, record how much time you spend in work activities (paid or unpaid and including household tasks) and pursuing your interests during downtime. Then examine it. If you are unsatisfied with how little time you devote to your interests, what small adjustments will you make?

23
JULY

I allow myself to follow my passions.

24
JULY
—

Our interests are an important part of who we are and can help us develop our sense of identity. This in turn helps us decide where we fit and with whom we want to interact. Write a brief bio or classified ad that tells others who you are based on your interests and passions. Take this to the next level by searching for interest groups of like-minded people.

25
JULY
—

Peruse magazines, catalogs, photographs, and other visual material. What piques your interest and generates feelings of excitement? Cut them out and create a collage. Give it an inspiring title, such as "Discovering My Interesting Life," and use it to create goals and actions.

26
JULY

Interests that are active (mentally or physically challenging) contribute to positive growth. What is one activity you could add to your life that would use or enhance some of your skills?

27
JULY

Mindfulness can help you get the most out of your interests and passions. This means paying attention fully to what you are doing and using all your senses to focus on your actions rather than the thoughts running through your mind. Mindfulness, though, is a personal endeavor. The next time you engage in a hobby or other activity, practice focusing your attention with one sense at a time. Notice sights, then sounds, then smells, and so on. Which sense is most vibrant to you and helps you stay interested and engaged? How can you use it more often?

28
JULY

Today, discover something new about yourself by exploring a new interest or pursuing an interest in a new way.

29
JULY

You can discover and develop your own passions by starting right where you are now. Make a list of daily tasks you don't mind doing. Pick one, perhaps cooking or shopping, and explore it more deeply. What is it about it that you enjoy, even slightly? Identify ways you could expand on it, allowing it to develop in new directions. Could you take a class (maybe a cooking class or a course about merchandising or the psychology of product packaging)? Where will that lead next?

30
JULY

Put your interests and passions to work for you by actively using them to shine. How will you know when you are shining?

31

JULY

"There is no passion to be found playing small—
in settling for a life that
is less than the one
you are capable of living."

—NELSON MANDELA

AUGUST

**Discovering My Goals,
Motivations, and Habits**

———————

1

AUGUST

Although we're motivated to meet our basic survival needs, we humans are capable of more than this. Pay attention to what motivates you to do what you're doing today, and why.

2

AUGUST

Go on an intentional walk—a mindful, motivational meandering. Notice what's happening around you as you move along your path, identify things that inspire and motivate you, and pay attention to how your mind and body react. For example, if you see the beauty of nature, are you motivated to volunteer for a park cleanup or to create or expand upon your own garden? If you see children playing at a school, are you motivated to become involved in a child's life or to take a class to learn something new?

3
AUGUST

"You can't just sit there and wait for
people to give you that golden dream.
You've got to get out there
and make it happen for yourself."

—DIANA ROSS

4
AUGUST

When you catch yourself dragging your feet on a project or other
endeavor, ask yourself whether you're pursuing your own goal or
someone else's.

5
AUGUST

Extrinsic motivation refers to driving forces outside of you. What rewards drive you (money, praise, success, winning, social media followers, etc.)? List as many rewards as you can in your notebook. Then reflect on their place in your life. How important are they to your sense of who you are? Are there some that you want to work harder toward? Any you want to let go?

6
AUGUST

Who or what motivates you to be a higher version of yourself? In what ways are you changing because of this person or idea?

7
AUGUST

Intrinsic motivation refers to the drive that comes from within you. You might do something for the sense of pleasure or satisfaction it brings, or because it aligns with your core values. In your notebook, describe the sense of satisfaction you receive from your work, spending time with loved ones, and attending to various responsibilities. If you received no tangible benefits from them (such as a paycheck or avoiding negative consequences), why would you keep doing them?

8
AUGUST

Healthy habits are meaningful actions we take so we can be the way we want to be in any situation. Do your lifestyle habits help or hinder you in being the person you want to be?

9
AUGUST

Stress has a way of zapping motivation. If you catch yourself feeling unmotivated today, try to identify the stressors you're facing. Think about what you need right now in order to better face them. This increased awareness of yourself and your stress is a powerful way to reclaim your zest.

10
AUGUST

"I see it feelingly."
—GLOUCESTER IN SHAKESPEARE'S *KING LEAR*; ACT 4, SCENE 6

11
AUGUST
—

Pause for a moment and think about what motivates you. Be present with it and try to feel your motivation with your whole body. What does it look like? Sound like? Feel like? Smell like? Taste like?

12
AUGUST
—

According to psychologist and researcher David Burns, action comes before motivation, not the other way around. In your notebook, reflect on your desires. Is there a goal you have but are feeling unmotivated to pursue it? Today, do one small action anyway. Then can you do one additional tiny thing? Notice how taking action despite a lack of motivation impacts your thoughts, feelings, and energy.

13
AUGUST
———

Motivation isn't just for the big stuff of life or reserved for lofty goals. You can learn a lot about yourself and strengthen your sense of contentment when you find motivation in the mundane. Why do you do all the myriad small things you do? Tune in to your deeper self today as you move through your day and identify reasons for what you are doing. Get basic and specific. When brushing your teeth, ask yourself, "Why *this* toothpaste?" Why do you choose the foods you prepare and eat? What drives you to behave in certain ways at work or with loved ones? What do these insights tell you about yourself?

14
AUGUST
———

I notice my habitual actions so
I make wise choices.

15

AUGUST

Engaging in habits mindfully rather than on autopilot allows you to replace automatic actions and reactions with skillful responses. Pay attention to one habit today, and take mindful actions.

16

AUGUST

Create a healthy habits jar to help you stay motivated and take small daily actions to build your habit. Think of a healthy habit you want to cultivate for yourself, and decide what encouragement and actions you need to build it. What words encourage you? What affirmations would be helpful to you? What actions would be meaningful and practical for you in your life? Write these self-encouragers on small slips of paper or on craft sticks, one item per paper or stick. Place them in an attractive, accessible jar or box, and establish a daily time (or multiple times) to draw one out. Do the action or repeat the affirmation to yourself.

17
AUGUST

———

Trying to make sweeping changes in your habits can be overwhelming. What is one small, problematic thing you habitually do?
What is one small, positive choice you could swap it for? Why not
start today?

18
AUGUST

———

When you purposefully discover your deeper motivations behind a goal, you
can then position yourself to take intentional action steps to work toward it. In
your notebook, write down a goal you have for your growth in one area of your
life. Next, describe what drives you toward this goal. List three to five actions
you will begin taking this week to advance toward it. How will your life be better
because of your dedication?

19

AUGUST

"Habits stay with you even when you don't have the motivation."

—NEERAJ AGNIHOTRI

20
AUGUST

If you're feeling unmotivated, is your lack of energy and enthusiasm related to something specific, or is it general? Review some of your personality traits you explored on January 3 (page 3). What can you draw on to give yourself a needed boost? In your journal, create an action plan for using these traits to motivate yourself.

21
AUGUST

Habits influence our thoughts, feelings, and level of motivation. Which of your habits help you think clearly, respond calmly to your emotions, and motivate you?

22
AUGUST

You can't force yourself to feel motivated with harsh and unkind words. However, you *can* nurture yourself and invite increased drive. Use the RAIN approach to self-love that you learned about on February 12 (page 30) to motivate yourself when needed: *Recognize* your level of motivation, *Allow* yourself to feel the way you do, *Investigate* to understand yourself and your feelings, and *Nurture* yourself with compassion for your slump. This approach leads to deeper self-understanding rather than self-criticism.

23
AUGUST

Consider your habits with honest openness. What bad habits are blocking you from being the person you want to be?

24
AUGUST

I identify my reasons for
doing what I do.

25
AUGUST

Create a vision board to help you maintain your motivation to cultivate healthy habits or to reach a specific goal. This could be a bulletin board on your wall, a specific app on your phone, or blank pages in a journal. Collect images and phrases that represent your habit/goal. Deepen your vision board by incorporating the things you are discovering about yourself—your traits, strengths, sense of meaning, etc. Revisit your collection every morning to pump you up for your day and shape the actions you will take toward this vision.

26
AUGUST

What obstacles are blocking your progress toward something you want? How driven are you to overcome these obstacles? What is one small step you can take today to move forward?

27
AUGUST

Pause frequently today to tune in to your body. What does it need to feel its best, inside and out? How will you fulfill those needs so you can remain motivated?

28

AUGUST

Notice your actions today in a new way. Pay attention to how your words and deeds, no matter how small they might seem at the time, and make a positive difference for yourself and others.

29

AUGUST

Today is a brand-new day. What would it be like for you to break the habit of living on autopilot, reacting to what comes your way, and instead approach it with renewed motivation?

30
AUGUST

My goals align with my vision for
who I want to be.

31
AUGUST

Imagine yourself in the future, after you've accomplished one of your current goals. Write a letter to your future self. Start by reminding this future self of how important this goal was to you when you were first beginning and why you were motivated to accomplish it. Tell yourself about all the obstacles you faced and what habits you created to overcome them. Describe what you've discovered about yourself in the process. Then speculate on how this future self will feel now that the goal is accomplished. End by expressing gratitude for all your hard work and perseverance.

SEPTEMBER

Discovering My Mind and Body

_____

1

SEPTEMBER

"When we bring awareness to our emotions . . .
they lose their power to make us miserable."

—DZOGCHEN PONLOP RINPOCHE

2

SEPTEMBER

The brain thinks between 2,100 and 3,300 thoughts an hour. About
70 percent are negative and automatic rather than purposeful.
Pause frequently today, and ask your brain what it's thinking so
you can intentionally shift.

3

SEPTEMBER

—

Explore your negative thoughts, and develop realistic alternatives to them. In your notebook, list several bothersome thoughts you have. While they feel completely accurate, it's likely that they're somewhat distorted. Consider each one and write several realistic alternatives. For example, "My boss hates me and I'll be fired" could shift to "My boss and I don't get along, but I do a good job" and "If I'm fired, I'll use my skills to find a better job."

4

SEPTEMBER

—

The human mind is on alert and often interprets situations as problematic. This causes negative thoughts and unpleasant feelings. Notice your moods today. Would you like a shift? Override your brain's hunt for problems by consciously hunting for positives.

5

SEPTEMBER

I carefully choose which thoughts
I pay attention to.

6

SEPTEMBER

Food and drink power our entire body and mind, influencing physical and mental health. Diets high in whole grains, vegetables, fruits, nuts, and seeds balance our moods and emotions, while diets low in these elements plus high in unhealthy fats, processed foods, and red meat have been found to contribute to anxiety, depression, and susceptibility to stress. For one week, track what you eat and record your emotions and thoughts as they pop into your mind. Discover patterns connecting your food and mood, and identify adjustments you might make.

7

SEPTEMBER

As you navigate your day, do you make choices without giving them much thought, or do you think about how big and little decisions affect your mind and body?

8

SEPTEMBER

The gut has been called our second brain, and it has its own nervous system. Actively notice how your gut responds to different situations, and let it increase your awareness of your emotional health.

9

SEPTEMBER

When you're experiencing a barrage of negative thoughts and unsettling emotions, do a quick body scan. Body scans not only help identify and release physical tension, but they also redirect the mind away from the intensity of problematic thoughts and feelings. Wherever you are, begin to breathe slowly and deeply. Starting at your feet and progressing though your body to the top of your head, focus on each muscle group, squeezing and releasing. How does the exercise help you?

10

SEPTEMBER

Today, practice noticing your thoughts and feelings without acting on them. Tonight, turn to your notebook and reflect on how delaying your reactions affected you.

11

SEPTEMBER

———

Studies show that when we face stressors, our thoughts and feelings about them are what activates our entire fight-flight-or-freeze reaction. Balancing our emotions and thoughts before we react can keep us centered and prevent the body from spiraling into the stress reaction. When you're upset, pause and breathe. Label your emotions, and allow yourself to feel this way. Remind yourself that you are in control and can choose how to respond.

12

SEPTEMBER

———

I notice and nurture my emotions

before they cause stress.

13
SEPTEMBER

Social media has a profound impact on our thoughts and emotions. When you're using it, notice how your mood changes. Could you give yourself a time limit, ending your session before your mood turns?

14
SEPTEMBER

Deep breathing helps you remain balanced by keeping your parasympathetic nervous system ("rest-and-digest") active and your sympathetic nervous system ("fight-flight-or-freeze") calm. This is because deep breathing signals the brain that you're okay despite difficulties you're dealing with. Developing the habit of breathing slowly and deeply helps maintain a balanced, healthy nervous system. Set an alarm to sound hourly, and when it chimes, check in with your breathing and take several long, slow, deep breaths.

15

Pay attention to what you do when you feel upset or have negative thoughts. What do you eat? Do you exercise or become sedentary? How do you relate to others? What might happen if you changed one of your go-to reactions?

16
SEPTEMBER

"The primary cause
of unhappiness is never
the situation but
your thoughts about it."

—ECKHART TOLLE

17

SEPTEMBER

Why not try scheduling time with your worries, fears, disappointments, and other such thoughts and feelings? For several days, set aside a specific time to devote to your negative thoughts and emotions. When they pop up at other times, remind yourself that you'll deal with them later. When the time comes, allow yourself to think about them for about 10 minutes before shifting to a new activity. After a few days, reflect on the experience. What was it like for you? Did you find it helpful?

18

SEPTEMBER

It's easy to become stuck in ruminations, which are repeated negative thoughts about problems. Create a positive thought loop instead. What are some positive thoughts that you can turn to when you catch yourself ruminating?

19

Meditation is a powerful healer: soothing every system in the body, focusing thoughts, and calming emotions. Try beginning and ending your day with this basic meditation. Sit comfortably, and gaze at something pleasing to you. As you inhale, think, *My mind is at ease.* As you exhale, think, *My body is relaxed.* When your mind wanders, return your attention to these phrases and the rhythm of your breath. As you practice, reflect on the experience in your notebook, and include new discoveries in how you feel mentally and physically (knowing that it takes time to notice the effects of meditation).

20

SEPTEMBER

—

Nature has a profound and positive effect on our well-being and has been shown to improve emotions and reduce negative ruminations. Create new outdoor rituals if your weather permits. You might step outside and take several deep breaths or go for a short walk. If you can't get out, bring nature inside with plants or a small water fountain. How might this make a positive difference for you?

21

SEPTEMBER

—

Moving your body can shake loose negative thoughts and feelings. What will you do today to purposefully move and shake?

22

SEPTEMBER

—

My choices help my body and mind
look out for each other.

23

SEPTEMBER

—

Give your thinking mind a break by turning to your body. What sensations do you notice on your skin? What scents does your nose pick up? What delights do your eyes spot? Grab a healthy bite and savor the taste and texture. Give yourself a chance to discover what your body likes, and practice providing it. When you let your body be in charge sometimes, your mind gets a reprieve.

24

SEPTEMBER

Research continues to uncover the deep connection between mind and body. Where do you feel your emotions in your body, and how does your body affect your mood?

25

SEPTEMBER

How are your eating habits? Do you often eat on the run or while doing other things like working or watching TV? Distracted eating perpetuates the body's stress reaction and impedes digestion. Think of your meals as a wonderful opportunity to nurture your body and shift your thoughts and emotions. Pick one meal a day, and approach it with intention for a week. Select healthy food and drink, and set aside time to sit down and savor it with no distraction. Note what the experience is like. What would it be like for you to continue past one week?

26
SEPTEMBER

Complete the sentence "I am _____" to explore who you are when your difficult thoughts, feelings, and physical sensations are not in the way.

27
SEPTEMBER

Negative thoughts and emotions are unpleasant, and it makes sense to want to avoid or ignore them. Doing this, though, can harm you. Ignoring them has a way of making them louder and more intense, plus they can expand into your body and cause headaches, digestive trouble, pain, illnesses, and more. Experiment to discover what helps you face and process your thoughts and emotions positively. Would you like to start a journal, visit with a trusted friend, see a therapist, join a support group, go to the gym regularly, or something else?

28
SEPTEMBER

Are you satisfied with the quality of your thoughts? What changes would you like to make? How will you be different when you make those changes?

29
SEPTEMBER

"Self-compassion is a more effective motivator than self-criticism because its driving force is love, not fear."

—KRISTIN NEFF

30
SEPTEMBER
—

Draw a tree in your notebook, including roots, branches, and leaves. Around the roots, write or draw representations of people and things that make you feel grounded and centered. Near the branches, write or draw what it is that you are reaching toward. Beside the leaves, write or draw what good you are absorbing from your world and how you are using it to nourish yourself. Now describe yourself as if you were a tree, with your thoughts, emotions, and body bending rather than breaking in the storms that come your way.

OCTOBER

Discovering Myself in
My Moments

———————

"It is impossible to become like somebody else. Your only hope is to become more fully yourself."

—JON KABAT-ZINN

2

OCTOBER

Settle in to a comfortable and pleasing spot today, and simply be. Don't pressure yourself to do anything. At the end of the day, consider what this was like for you and what you learned about yourself in doing nothing.

3

OCTOBER

While setting and working toward goals is a healthy part of life and growth, it is just as important to practice what in mindfulness is known as non-striving. It's a new way of being with and seeing yourself. Self-discovery isn't about becoming a better person. Instead, it's about getting to know and being comfortable with who you are. Write encouraging notes to yourself, perhaps drawn from other reflections and exercises in this book, that remind you of the wonderful things you're learning about yourself. Place them where you'll notice them frequently.

4

OCTOBER

Who guides you to find the right direction? Yourself? Or do you more frequently follow the direction of others? Would you like more balance between the two?

5
OCTOBER

Breathing exercises can help you notice and become nonjudgmental and patient with the activity of your mind. Get comfortable, and breathe slowly and deeply. Notice where in your body you feel your breath the most, and anchor your attention there. When your thoughts go off in a different direction, neither stop nor follow them. Just patiently keep returning to your breath's anchor point in your body. How can you use this exercise for your own benefit in daily life?

6
OCTOBER

Acceptance lets you say, "Yes, problem, I know you're there. I'm going to just let you be there while I go forward and create the life I want to live." What will you go forward with today?

7

OCTOBER

In the process of self-discovery, it helps to free yourself from fighting your obstacles. When you accept that they exist, you can turn your thoughts and energy to other things. In your notebook, describe a problem you're facing and list your thoughts and emotions about it. Sit with these thoughts and feelings while you breathe slowly and deeply. Let them exist, and then expand your attention. What do you notice about this moment? What's around you and inside of you? What positive action can you take right now to build on these other things?

8

OCTOBER

I let go of my resistance to difficulty and focus on myself and the good in the moment.

9

OCTOBER

In your notebook, write about something that bothered you recently. What were your dominant ideas about it? What actions did you take because of them, and how quickly did you take them? Do you think you could face a challenging situation and let it be as it is, without immediately acting on it? How might you benefit from patiently waiting before acting?

10

OCTOBER

Part of living mindfully means taking control of your attention and where you want to place it. Pledge to pay full attention to each task today, no matter what that task may be. Then consider how this affected you.

11

OCTOBER

Do you go through your day on autopilot, distracted with a wandering mind? Researchers link autopilot to unhappiness. Do your own version of a 2010 Harvard study: Set your phone alarm to chime at random times throughout your day, at least six times. When it sounds, pause and record your level of happiness, what you are doing, and what you are thinking about (your current activity or something else). Look for patterns. How much time do you spend distracted, and how does this affect your mood?

12

OCTOBER

Do you tend to be patient, letting things happen in their own time, or impatient, wanting to control each moment? How does your level of patience serve you?

13

OCTOBER

Which do you find yourself focusing on more: Problems from the past or possibilities of your future? Experiment with a focus on developing possibilities for yourself right now, and see how it affects your energy.

14

OCTOBER

Have a mealtime conversation with loved ones or coworkers about what is going well today. Take turns sharing at least one thing that you have done well or enjoyed today. When each person is talking, give them your full attention rather than interrupting or being distracted, and when you're sharing, be specific and speak from your heart. Later, reflect in your notebook. What was this like? What new insights did you discover about yourself and your day that you'll carry forward into tomorrow?

15
OCTOBER
—

"In the beginner's mind there
are many possibilities, but in the
expert's mind there are few."

—SHUNRYŪ SUZUKI

16
OCTOBER
—

An important component of mindfulness, beginner's mind, means approaching each situation with openness and nonjudgment, as if you were completely
new to it. You can use beginner's mind toward yourself, too. Stand in front of a
mirror and study yourself as if you were a stranger. Describe this person with a
fresh, neutral perspective. As you go about your day, pretend you are shadow-
ing someone you just met. Just witness what you observe about this person
(yourself) in the present.

17

OCTOBER

Practice noticing new sights, sounds, smells, and tastes throughout your day. Notice how new discoveries affect your mood and energy.

18

OCTOBER

I meet each situation as it is rather than burdening myself with judgments.

19
OCTOBER

Judging our experiences as good or bad distorts them. Pay close attention to how much you do it. Reword judgmental statements to be neutral. How do your emotions and perspective change?

20
OCTOBER

Yoga can teach you to listen to and trust yourself. Sitting on the edge of a chair, place your right hand on your left knee. Inhale deeply. As you exhale, slowly twist to the left, placing your left hand behind you and looking over your left shoulder. Repeat on the other side. Notice sensations in your body, and stop if something hurts. In your daily tasks and interactions, do you stop when something hurts? Practice bringing the body awareness of yoga to other areas of your life.

21
OCTOBER
—

Catch your feelings of frustration toward yourself when you're stressed, and recognize this as a habitual pattern of judging. Let that realization be there, and then shift your focus by immediately acknowledging your progress.

22
OCTOBER
—

Social media encourages us to "like" and "dislike" everything, but imposing value judgments confines us and makes it hard to experience inner peace. Take a break from social media today and practice being a neutral observer in your real world. Carry your notebook with you, and pause periodically to observe and describe what is happening in the moment. Is it hard to describe things without using value judgments? What might happen to your outlook if you started doing this often?

23
OCTOBER

It's easy to let small, everyday moments pass by unnoticed or unappreciated. When this happens, we miss out on a lot of our lives. Practice these two things today to savor your life a moment at a time. First, instead of multitasking, give your full attention to the task at hand. Second, pause to celebrate little joys as they happen. High-five someone, do a little dance, treat yourself to a mindful walk or healthy snack—and savor these celebrations, too. Later, use your journal to reflect on your experience and how it enriched you.

24
OCTOBER

I pay attention to myself in each moment
and give myself what I need.

25

OCTOBER

Shenpa is a Buddhist concept referring to getting hooked on something. Go fishing without your hook today. Actively discover when you're stuck in challenges and then, with intent, choose to take an action away from them.

26

OCTOBER

How does holding on to difficulties from the past or concerns about the future affect you emotionally and physically? What would be different if you released them, concentrating instead on how you feel in the present moment?

27

OCTOBER

How do you see yourself? Is your opinion clouded by what Deepak Chopra has called "outworn memories" from the past? What would it be like to give yourself a fresh start today?

28

OCTOBER

—

When you become aware that you have lost your sense of self during a stressful day, perhaps because you are caught in judging, resisting, or people-pleasing, pause where you are and turn inward. Repeat this meditative gatha several times and feel yourself reconnecting to the inner you:

Breathing in, I am aware of my mind and body.

Breathing out, I accept myself and the moment fully.

Breathing in, I let go of harsh judgments.

Breathing out, I know who I am and I value myself.

29
OCTOBER

When you're not stressed and pressured, what is it like to be in your body? What is happening in your mind? Describe this feeling deeply and specifically so that you can evoke it even in difficult, stressful moments. Write a detailed description of yourself in a state of equanimity, and then turn it into a visualization exercise you can recite to yourself in moments of agitation. Use "I am" statements, such as "I am loose. I am free from stomach pain. I am detached."

30
OCTOBER

Today, pay attention to the sounds around you and use them as cues to discover your moment more deeply and yourself in it.

31

OCTOBER

"If we are not fully
ourselves, truly in
the present moment,
we miss everything."

—THÍCH NHẤT HẠNH

NOVEMBER

Discovering My Sense of Gratitude

_____

1
NOVEMBER

I am thankful for my ongoing
self-discovery process.

2
NOVEMBER

Throughout your day, pause and let your gaze fall on a random object. Study it without judging it, and notice what memories it evokes. What about the object and memories make you glad and grateful? What were you like in that memory? How can you reawaken that part of you today?

3

NOVEMBER

Gratitude is a way of experiencing yourself and your life. Observe yourself today, and purposefully notice and appreciate many aspects of yourself. Express appreciation to yourself for yourself.

4

NOVEMBER

Look for reasons to be grateful today, but don't stop with this noticing. Use it to learn about yourself and probe, "Why am I grateful for this? What is it that resonates with me?"

5

NOVEMBER

Feeling grateful doesn't mean glossing over problems and challenges. Instead, it's awareness of what is wrong and still believing that many things are right with yourself and your life. This awareness isn't always easy. How difficult is it for you to focus on what is right amid a host of obstacles? Reflect on this honestly in your notebook, knowing that it isn't a judgment on your character but a way of exploring yourself to gain clarity into your own unique perspective.

6

NOVEMBER

"As we express our gratitude, we must never forget that the highest appreciation is not to utter words, but to live by them."

—JOHN F. KENNEDY

7

NOVEMBER

For you, is gratitude more about your outlook on life or shaping the actions you take? In what ways can you make it be about both?

8

NOVEMBER

Play gratitude bingo. Create a bingo card and fill all the squares with people, places, things, and your own personality and strengths that make you feel grateful. Be on alert for these things, and mark them off your card as you go. When you've achieved blackout bingo (you've checked off everything on your card), treat yourself to something you enjoy and consider how this activity has impacted your sense of self in the world.

9
NOVEMBER

"Gratitude helps you to grow and expand;
gratitude brings JOY and laughter into your life
and into the lives of all those around you."

—EILEEN CADDY

10
NOVEMBER

Gratitude won't directly fix a problem, but it can alter how we
view it, freeing us to act intentionally. Discover how finding one
thing to be grateful for in a difficult situation changes your outlook and choices.

11
NOVEMBER

Apply this well-researched exercise from positive psychology into your own bedtime routine and start a gratitude journal. Select a special journal or notebook for this purpose, and each night before going to sleep, write down three good things from your day. Be sure to include things about yourself for which you are grateful (personality traits, values, actions, strengths, how you are in relationships, etc.) to help you discover and appreciate yourself.

12
NOVEMBER

The more you look for the good in yourself and your life, the more you will find. Today, seek gratitude in everything and pay attention to how your mood and outlook shift.

13

NOVEMBER

When you can't seem to shake negative thoughts or emotions about a difficulty you're facing, immediately do this on-the-spot meditation as you are and wherever you are.

Begin to breathe slowly and deeply, visualizing your breaths as ocean waves.

Let your thoughts drift by, neither trying to stop nor change them.

Pluck one thought from the flow, and begin to think about it in a new way, bringing a sense of gratitude to what it represents. Perhaps you're grateful that you care about it or that you have skills to deal with it.

Continue to breathe and bring gratitude to mind as long as you wish.

14
NOVEMBER

What might cultivating gratitude do for your sense of self and how you approach life?

15
NOVEMBER

Gratitude can be difficult to feel and express. Stress can give us tunnel vision and be depleting, making it difficult to muster energy for gratitude. Also, it's common to feel guilty for being grateful in the midst of so many difficulties in the world. Discovering your own roadblocks to gratitude can help. In your notebook, reflect on your own relationship with gratitude. How easy or difficult is it to feel it? Why? What is one thing you can do to enhance or continue your sense of gratitude?

16
NOVEMBER

Put an active twist on grateful feelings today. Notice what you're grateful for in order to gain insights into what you want more of in your life. What action step will you take today to build on it?

17
NOVEMBER

Revisit the bothersome thoughts you explored on September 3 (page 165). This time, see if you can change your relationship with the thoughts and the situations they represent. For each thought, identify something about the situation or your own approach to it that you feel grateful about. How does looking at a negative thought or bothersome situation through a lens of gratitude make a difference in how you feel about it and yourself?

18
NOVEMBER
———

I choose to appreciate the good in every situation.

19
NOVEMBER
———

Keep a container and a stack of index cards in a prominent living space. Develop the habit of looking for things big and small for which you are grateful. In the moment, jot them down and place it in the container. Establish a regular time, perhaps every Sunday night before starting your new week, to revisit your notes and re-experience your gratitude for these moments. This can teach you a lot about yourself and what's important to you.

20

How can your sense of gratitude help you problem-solve today? What new perspectives can it bring to a challenge you're facing?

21

Rather than using gratefulness as a convenience, expressing it only in good times or using it here and there to change your perspective, cultivate it as one of your core personality traits, an integral part of who you are. Start each new day by setting an intention to pause at regular intervals (you determine what works for you—once in the morning and once in the afternoon, every hour, etc.) and appreciate one thing about yourself and one thing about the moment.

22

NOVEMBER

—

In what ways does cultivating a greater sense of gratitude deepen your connection with yourself, others, and something greater than yourself?

23

NOVEMBER

—

"Being thankful is not always experienced as a natural state of existence, we must work at it, akin to a type of strength training for the heart."

—LARISSA GOMEZ

24

NOVEMBER

———

At a store or other public place, make a point to thank someone for something small. Perhaps ask a random person where an item is, and then look at them and thank them for helping you. Try this and watch the transformation—in the other person or within yourself. What would it be like to commit to doing this every day? Try it for at least one week, and evaluate how your perspective and energy shift.

25
NOVEMBER

Try infusing upsetting emotions with an underlying sense of gratitude today. How might you temper anger with gratefulness, for example? What does this do for your sense of inner balance?

26
NOVEMBER

How do you feel and react when you have to slow down and wait? Impatient? Bored? These are normal human reactions; however, you don't have to be at their mercy. Make these times entertaining and allow them to help you discover a deeper awareness of your gratitude. Challenge yourself by seeing how many things you can spot that remind you of something you're grateful for. Keep a running total and try to set and beat personal records.

27

NOVEMBER

As you pondered on October 6 (page 187), acceptance means letting a difficulty exist while proceeding with your life. How can you use your own sense of gratitude to accept challenges more easily?

28

NOVEMBER

Create a gratitude coloring book or folder by purchasing gratitude coloring books, printing free online pages, or draw your own outlines to color in. Settle into a comfortable, quiet space, play music you love, and set the mood with lighting, candles, plants, photos, and other objects. As you color, reflect on your deep sense of gratitude. This form of meditation can create a powerful shift in your mood and emotions. Notice what it does for you.

29
NOVEMBER
—

Openly share your gratitude with a loved one today, paying attention to what this does for your mood, thoughts, emotions, and sense of connection.

30
NOVEMBER
—

I am grateful for all that I am.

DECEMBER

Discovering My Character Strengths

_____

1

"The most authentic thing about us is
our capacity to create, to overcome,
to endure, to transform, to love and to
be greater than our suffering."

—BEN OKRI

2

DECEMBER

Extensive research has named and identified key character strengths that we draw on in every situation in life. Embark on a journey of identifying your own. Observe yourself today, and begin to compile a list of qualities you possess. If you'd like, you can draw inspiration from VIA Institute on Character, a research organization dedicated to helping people understand and use their strengths. Find them in the Resources section at the end of this book (page 239).

3

DECEMBER

As you discover your unique strengths and ways of using them, avoid value judgments. No strength is "better" than another. Observe and appreciate your character strengths without assessing them.

4

DECEMBER

Courage is considered a strength and includes traits such as perseverance and honesty. How do you show courage, and how can you use it today to accomplish something important to you?

5

DECEMBER

Use this gatha each morning to help encourage you to let your strengths guide you as you navigate the day. Do this every day for one week, and reflect on the experience in your notebook. How much did it help you realize and use more of your strengths?

Breathing in, I know that I have strengths.

Breathing out, I embrace the process of discovering them.

Drawing on the uniqueness of my own character,

I lead with my strengths in all situations.

6
DECEMBER

I focus on my many strengths with pride.

7
DECEMBER

How important are the strengths of curiosity and creativity to you in daily life?

8
DECEMBER

It is a strength to show kindness and recognize the humanity in yourself and others. How much do you tend-and-befriend yourself and the people you encounter?

9
DECEMBER

You can use strengths to relate to others. How do you draw on leadership skills or a sense of fairness in daily activities?

10

DECEMBER

Everyone possesses some capacity for forgiveness and self-regulation (the ability to resist impulses). How prominent are they for you?

11

DECEMBER

Character strengths are separate from personality traits, but there is overlap between them. Consider the Big Five traits you discovered about yourself on January 3 (page 3). List the traits and associated words that fit you. Now think about them through the lens of your character strengths. How are your strengths mirrored in your unique traits?

12

DECEMBER

Our sense of who we are involves not just our traits, actions, or work but also an idea of where we fit in the bigger picture of life. Some people connect with religious beliefs, while others find greater meaning elsewhere. How is your sense of self influenced by the idea of a bigger picture?

13

DECEMBER

We can use our unique strengths to solve problems or find motivation to persevere. Write about something you are having a difficult time finding the motivation to do. Which of your strengths could you draw on to get it done?

14
DECEMBER

—

"Both the head and the heart
strengths are important to our
being well-rounded people."

—RYAN NIEMIEC

15
DECEMBER

—

Implement a "Strength of the Day" plan. Every morning, reflect on a trait that
makes you strong, and keep this quality in mind as you move through your day.
How can you use it intentionally in your roles and responsibilities, as well as your
ups and downs?

16
DECEMBER

Which of your strengths might serve you best in your interactions with others and with yourself today?

17
DECEMBER

Go on a strengths-spotting safari. In every interaction you have with someone today, whether that's a loved one, neighbor, colleague, or clerk at a store, watch for the strengths they exhibit. For example, was someone particularly kind? Did they show curiosity, humility, or humor? How did this alter your perspective about others? How will viewing others this way change something in you?

18

In your notebook, describe a stressor you are facing right now in your life. How is it affecting your thoughts, emotions, physical health, actions, and relationships? Now list some things about yourself that you're proud of. Look at your list and consider which of your strengths are shining through, and write a brief action plan that involves using that strength to move forward and ultimately past your stressor.

19

Think about your interests and passions, and consider how you approach and engage in them. What insights do they give you into some of your strengths?

20

DECEMBER

In your notebook, write your own gatha to use daily. As I mentioned on April 16 (page 73), a gatha is a short meditation consisting of two or four lines that is designed to help you reflect on a concept as you inhale and exhale to the rhythm of the lines. Pick a personal strength and incorporate it into a short meditation that you can repeat often to remind yourself of this positive personal quality.

21

DECEMBER

Sometimes we overuse a strength, drawing on it heavily without balancing it with our other strengths. Notice your strengths in action today, and check to see if this is happening with you. How might you find balance with a rarely used strength?

22
DECEMBER

—

I trust my strengths to guide my actions.

23
DECEMBER

—

Our strengths are believed to come from our genes as well as things we learn as we grow and develop throughout our lives. To gain deeper insight into your own strengths, think about the people who have influenced you. What strengths do they possess that you now see in yourself? If possible, consider sharing your observations with one or more of these people. What strengths would you draw on to have such a discussion?

24
DECEMBER

"True happiness comes . . . when we see
our problems as a potential source of awakening,
opportunities to practice patience, and to learn."

—RICHARD CARLSON

25
DECEMBER

Use your strengths to deepen your sense of purpose and meaning. Consider
what you've discovered about yourself. Write a personal mission statement
declaring how you will draw on your strengths to enrich your life.

26

DECEMBER

Character strengths are very much about actions. How do your strengths shine in the things you do, big and small, every day?

27

DECEMBER

How are you able to manifest your character strengths at work (paid or unpaid)? To what extent do you feel fulfilled by incorporating strengths into your work?

28
DECEMBER

———

Learn more about yourself by drawing on the perspective of others in your life. Ask friends, family members, maybe even coworkers. Then compile them, tracking the different strengths people see in you. Which ones are chosen by several people? What new insights did you gain into yourself from this exercise?

29
DECEMBER

———

I am powerfully responsible for myself and my life.

30
DECEMBER

Now, at the end of your year, what is your vision of your best possible self? Write a description of you at your very best, free to be your authentic self. Are you able now to appreciate all of the rich, varied, and complex aspects of you? Show yourself some love, appreciation, and respect in this description, honoring all that you are and all that you do.

31
DECEMBER

"What we must try to be, of course, is ourselves and wholeheartedly. We must find out what we really are and what we really want."

—NELSON BOSWELL

Resources

If you are interested in continuing your self-discovery journey, you may find these resources to be helpful companions.

WEBSITES

American Institute of Stress: Stress.org. The authority on stress and stress management, Stress.org offers extensive articles, videos, webinars, and a podcast to help you deal positively with stress and challenge in a way that suits you.

Truity: Truity.com/test/big-five-personality-test. Take free personality tests, including the Big Five trait assessment and career assessments, to help you align your personality with a meaningful career.

VIA Institute on Character: VIACharacter.org. Discover your own character strengths profile with this free assessment. Read a wealth of articles to learn how to apply your strengths to your life.

BOOKS

Break Free: Acceptance and Commitment Therapy in 3 Steps by Tanya J. Peterson. Explore your own values and develop a personal action plan to thrive despite obstacles.

Coming to Our Senses: Healing Ourselves and the World through Mindfulness by Jon Kabat-Zinn. Explore the concept of mindfulness and learn how to enrich your own life by living mindfully.

Flow by Mihaly Csikszentmihalyi. Explore the concept of flow in order to find your unique interests and passions that help you achieve this state of well-being.

The Healing Self: A Revolutionary New Plan to Supercharge Your Immunity and Stay Well for Life by Deepak Chopra and Rudolph E. Tanzi. Learn more about your mind and body, and develop your own unique plan for health and well-being by choosing activities that fit you and your life.

Real Love: The Art of Mindful Connection by Sharon Salzberg. Discover why you really do deserve your own love, and learn to treat yourself with the loving-kindness you deserve.

References

American Institute of Stress. "Mismatched: Your Brain Under Stress." Accessed September 14, 2021. Stress.org/mismatched-your-brain-under-stress.

American Institute of Stress. "The Role of Emotion in Stress." *Finding Contentment* podcast. September 7, 2021. Accessed September 2021. Podcast audio. Bit.ly/3AJ7ptG.

Appalachian State University Center for Academic Excellence. "Big 8 Identities." Accessed September 16, 2021. CAE.AppState.edu/sites/cae.appstate.edu/files/big-8-identities.pdf.

Brach, Tara. "Feeling Overwhelmed? Remember 'RAIN.'" *Mindful.* February 7, 2019. Mindful.org/tara-brach-rain-mindfulness-practice.

Brinker, J.K., Z. H. Chin, and R. Wilkinson. "Ruminative Thought Style and Personality." *Personality and Individual Differences* 60, Supplement (April 2014): S41. doi.org/10.1016/j.paid.2013.07.112.

Chamorro-Premuzic, Thomas, and Adrian Furnham. "Personality and Music: Can Traits Explain How People Use Music in Everyday Life?" *British Journal of Psychology* 98, no. 2 (December 2010): 175–85. doi.org/10.1348/000712606X111177.

Chopra, Deepak, and Rudolph E. Tanzi. *The Healing Self: A Revolutionary New Plan to Supercharge Your Immunity and Stay Well for Life.* New York: Harmony Books, 2020.

Clapp, Megan, Nadia Aurora, Lindsey Herrera, Manisha Bhatia, Emily Wilen, and Sarah Wakefield. "Gut Microbiota's Effect on Mental Health: The Gut-Brain Axis." *Clinics and Practice* 7, no. 4 (September 15, 2017): 131–6. doi.org/10.4081/cp.2017.987.

Colier, Nancy. "Why Your Thoughts Are Not Real." *Psychology Today.* August 23, 2013. PsychologyToday.com/us/blog/inviting-monkey-tea/201308/why-your-thoughts-are-not-real.

Csikszentmihalyi, Mihaly. *Flow: The Psychology of Optimal Experience.* New York: Harper Perennial Modern Classics, 2008.

Daniels, Patricia. *Your Personality Explained: Exploring the Science of Identity.* Washington, DC: National Geographic Society, 2014.

Germer, Christopher K., and Kristin D. Neff. "Self-Compassion in Clinical Practice." *Journal of Clinical Psychology* 69, no. 8 (August 2013): 856–67. doi: 10.1002/jclp.22021.

Jagoo, Krystal. "Even with Exercise, Sedentary Lifestyle Has Consequences for Mental Health." Verywell Mind. August 25, 2021. VerywellMind.com/study-suggests-sitting-has-negative-impact-on-mental-health-5195714.

Harvard Medical School, "The Gut-Brain Connection." Harvard Health Publishing. April 19, 2021. Health.Harvard.edu/diseases-and-conditions/the-gut-brain-connection.

Kabat-Zinn, Jon. *Coming to Our Senses: Healing Ourselves and the World through Mindfulness.* New York: Hachette Books, 2005.

Katsumi, Yuta, Ekaterina Denkova, and Sanda Dolcos. "Personality and Memory." In *Encyclopedia of Personality and Individual Differences,* edited by Virgil Zeigler-Hill and Todd K. Shackelford. New York: Springer International Publishing, 2017.

Killingsworth, Matthew A., and Daniel T. Gilbert. "A Wandering Mind Is an Unhappy Mind." *Science* 330, no. 6006 (November 12, 2010): 932. doi.org/10.1126/science.1192439.

Magill, Amy. "What Is the Relationships between Food and Mood?" Mental Health First Aid. March 13, 2018. MentalHealthFirstAid.org/external/2018/03/relationship-food-mood.

Marano, Hara Estroff. "Our Brain's Negative Bias." *Psychology Today.* Last reviewed June 9, 2016. PsychologyToday.com/us/articles/200306/our-brains-negative-bias.

McCraty, Rollin, Bob Barrios-Choplin, Mike Atkinson, and Dana Tomasino. "The Effects of Different Types of Music on Mood, Tension, and Mental Clarity." *Alternative Therapies* 4, no. 1 (January 1998): 75–84. HeartMath.org/assets/uploads/2015/01/music-mood-effects.pdf.

McKenzie, Jessica. "Loving Your Job Matters." *Good Company* 12, no. 2 (February 21, 2018). APAExcellence.org/resources/goodcompany /newsletter/article/860.

Niemiec, Ryan M. *Mindfulness & Character Strengths: A Practical Guide to Flourishing.* Boston: Hogrefe Publishing, 2014.

Peterson, Sarah J., Daryl R. Van Tongeren, Stephanie D. Womack., Joshua N. Hook, Don E. Davis., and Brandon J. Griffin. "The Benefits of Self-Forgiveness on Mental Health: Evidence from Correlational and Experimental Research." *The Journal of Positive Psychology* 12, no. 2 (2017): 159–68. doi.org/10.1080/17439760.2016.1163407.

Pillay, Sirini. "Greater Self-Acceptance Improves Emotional Well-Being." *Harvard Health Blog.* May 16, 2016. Health.Harvard.edu/blog/greater -self-acceptance-improves-emotional-well-201605169546.

Psychology Today Staff. "Big 5 Personality Traits." *Psychology Today.* Accessed September 14, 2021. PsychologyToday.com/us/basics/big-5 -personality-traits.

Psychology Today Staff. "Identity." *Psychology Today.* Accessed September 10, 2021. PsychologyToday.com/us/basics/identity.

Salzberg, Sharon. *Real Love: The Art of Mindful Connection.* New York: Flatiron Books, 2017.

Salzberg, Sharon. "Why Loving-Kindness Takes Time: Sharon Salzberg." *Mindful*. January 19, 2018. Mindful.org/loving-kindness-takes-time -sharon-salzberg.

Schulenberg, Stefan E., Robert R. Hutzell, Carrie Nassif, and Julius Rogina. "Logotherapy for Clinical Practice." *Psychotherapy Theory Research Practice Training* 45, no. 4 (December 2008): 447–63. doi.org/10.1037 /a0014331.

Seligman, Martin E. P. *Flourish*. New York: Atria Books, 2011.

Sharf, Richard S. *Applying Career Development Theory to Counseling*. 4th ed. Belmont, CA: Thomson Brooks/Cole, 2006.

Smith, Martin M., Slmon B. Sherry, Samanth Chen, Donald H. Saklofske, Christopher Mushquash, Gordon L. Flett, and Paul L. Hewitt. "The Perniciousness of Perfectionism: A Meta-Analytic Review of the Perfectionism–Suicide Relationship. *Journal of Personality* 86, no. 3 (June 2018): 522–42. doi.org/10.1111/jopy.12333.

Strauss Cohen, Ilene. "How to Let Go of the Need for Approval and Live the Life You Want." *Psychology Today*. July 13, 2018. PsychologyToday.com /us/blog/your-emotional-meter/201807/how-let-go-the-need-approval.

UPMC Health Beat. "Managing Ruminating Thoughts for Better Mental Health." UPMC Western Behavioral Health. Last reviewed October 23, 2020. Share.UPMC.com/2020/10/ruminating-thoughts.

Index

ACKNOWLEDGMENTS

Thank you to Carolyn Abate, my editor who helped make this book a useful resource for anyone embarking on a journey of self-discovery. I'm also grateful for the entire Callisto Media team, a very talented group that publishes outstanding, life-enhancing books. Thank you for allowing me to contribute.

ABOUT THE AUTHOR

 Tanya J. Peterson, MS, NCC, holds a master of science degree in counseling, is credentialed by the National Board of Certified Counselors, and is a diplomate of the American Institute of Stress (AIS). She is the author of 10 self-help books and a regular contributor to a variety of mental health websites. Formerly a teacher and school counselor, Peterson has also created a mental health course for kids. Peterson has delivered a webinar for the AIS, participated in expert panels, appeared on numerous podcasts and other interview shows, and been quoted in a variety of online articles. She's been featured twice in Authority Magazine regarding developing healthy habits for well-being and leveraging the power of gratitude for wellness. Her work centers on helping people understand and build mindfulness skills in order to live fully in each moment, rather than stuck in their thoughts and feelings about problematic situations.

CPSIA information can be obtained
at www.ICGtesting.com
Printed in the USA
JSHW021437040322
23601JS00001B/1

9 781638 076575